My Turkish Missile Crisis

A Memoir from the Frontline of October 1962

Joseph Maiolo

Overcoat **Books**

Duluth, Minnesota

Overcoat Books
An imprint of X-Communication
118 Chester Parkway
Duluth, Minnesota 55805
218-310-6541

My Turkish missile crisis: a memoir from the frontline of October 1962

Cover photograph and the photograph of the
jupiter missile on page 20 courtesy George Smith

Map of Turkey on page 12 by
Peter Fitzgerald courtesy wikitravel.com

Unless otherwise noted, all other
photos are the property of the author

The author was aided by the following publications:

Thirteen Days: A Memoir of the Cuban Missile Crisis
by Robert F. Kennedy (W. W. Norton, New York, 1973)

*Transcriptions of the deliberations of the Executive Committee of the
National Security Council (EX-COMM) during the Cuban Missile
Crisis: October 16-28, 1962* (Transcribed Audio Files,
U.S. Government, 21 August 1997, Revised 8 October 1997)

First Edition, 2011

12 13 14 15 16 • 5 4 3 2 1

Library of Congress Control Number: 2011943231

Softcover ISBN: 978-1-887317-90-0

Printed in the U.S.A.

For Julie
in memory and in love

~

Also by Joseph Maiolo and Overcoat Books:

Boy • *Youth* • *Man* (a triptych of novellas)

I have set out to tell about a potentially
cataclysmic set of world events, at whose center
I found myself when I was a young man in whom
significance resided primarily in how events affected me,
or failed to. Now I see that my arrival in Turkey and,
thirteen months later, my departure would serve as
symbolic bookends for one enormous story:
The World in the Balance, and Again.

— J. M.

ITALY

THE TRUE STORY BEGINS IN SOUTHERN ITALY, in the Sila Mountains of Calabria, where I had gone to Gimigliano, the destitute village of my grandmother's birth and girlhood, to visit her aging brother.

As I sat shaving before a pan of water and a piece of mirror, the children came, watching me from the open doorway and, soon, whispering: *"Americani volano bene a uovi"* (Americans love eggs). And so they went, as if on an Easter-morning hunt.

I was surprised when they returned so soon. There had been three or four of them earlier. Now they were a small crowd, bearing the treasure—a single egg—worth perhaps ten thousand *lire*. Their faces alight with great smiles, they presented the delicacy to me, I accepted it, turned to my great uncle, and asked if I should try to pay them something. His head went up slightly and he jerked it, closing his eyes briefly and making a mouth sound—*tsk*—in one of the numerous gestures I was beginning to read. (I knew several from my grandmother back in Virginia.) No, they would not accept any payment. They had prevailed upon an old widow to contribute the treasure in homage to the visitor to the village—me—and so, out of respect, it was a small gift to America itself.

"*Troppo ricca*," Uncle Raffaele said, mock-slapping at his ear: The widow was very rich.

In the evening a hobo of a man came to the doorway with a sweet look on his dirty face and sang a version of "*Core 'Ngrato*." I did not need to ask my great uncle's advice about the *lire* I gave him.

That night Great Aunt Carmella said that she would sleep on the cot in the kitchen-sitting area, so that Uncle Raffaele and I could have the bed. I could not convince her that her discomfort would make me feel guilty without calling attention to her being lame and aged, and there was no argument to be made anyway.

"*Dorma*," she said in her rasping voice. Sleep.

By the time I settled into the concave mattress, I must have fallen into a deep, dreamless oblivion. Sometime later, I woke with the movement of someone in bed with me, and wondered briefly where I was.

"*Giusse*," Uncle Raffaele whispered. "*Sta dormindo*"?

"No, I'm awake." I spoke (during my two weeks there), haltingly, in the "proper" Italian I had studied in college, not Uncle Raffaele's and my grandmother's dialect, Calabrese, much of which I could understand, but not speak so well.

He told me a story about when he was a boy and one of his older sisters, Angelica, who would be my maternal grandmother, took him with her when she went into the mountains to gather wood. The blight that would leave only scattered chestnut trees had not hit yet, so she filled his pockets and shirt front with the nuts, then gathered and tied a bundle of branches to carry on her head for firewood. But he sprained his ankle, and so she had to carry him on her back and he carried the wood on his head. He said he must have looked like a "*scoiattolo*."

"*Che vuol dire, 'scoiattolo'*" (What does *scoiattolo* mean)?

The moon providing a spotlight, he squinched his mouth up and chattered.

"Ah," I said. "Squirrel."

He said the word slowly, in attempted imitation, his *r*'s slurred gutturally. My attempt to stifle the laugh coming from my throat only made what did issue a surely demented-sounding guffaw, and I clamped a hand over my mouth. I might as well have been trying to compress a balloon without bursting it.

That set him off, and he set me off again, and we laughed most of that night away (and much of the other nights to come). When one of us moved a foot or elbow and we touched, the other one might give just a half-laugh, and soon we were gasping, stuffing our mouths with the blanket to keep from waking Aunt Carmella. But nothing could stanch our jubilant foolery. Once it got going, we were reduced to giggling boys.

In the morning we drank what Uncle Raffaele called "*'na dram-a*" of *grappa*, then broke hunks from a breadloaf to eat with our *espresso*. I took a Winston from my box and gave him one (he tore off the filter), flipped up the top of my shiny Zippo and popped the flint with my thumb, then lit our cigarettes and snapped the top down. (It was a one-handed routine I'd learned as a boy from men in my town who'd returned from the war with the lighter made famous by Ernie Pyle and G. I. Joe.) Uncle Raffaele tried doing it, but fumbled, made a gesture of screwing a finger into his cheek, and we laughed.

Gradually, though, his face went solemn; his eyes glistened into prominence. A boy from the village had been shot in his foxhole while lighting a cigarette at night, he told me, and we sat there in mute homage, looking at the famous lighter.

He was going hunting this morning. Whenever he killed a fox, he received a small bounty and sold the fur for a few thousand *lire*. He took the rifle down from over the front doorway and began to inspect it; with its hexagonal outer barrel, ornate hammer, and what looked like rough pinewood stock, it called to my mind a musket.

He asked me if I hunted, and I tried to tell him about the time I'd begun quaking when I'd sighted in on my first and only quarry. The guys with me told everybody I'd not even got buck fever, because I'd sighted in on a doe. But I couldn't quite get the story across to my great uncle, a veteran of World War One, as he stood before me with his antiquated gun, hopeful of bagging a fox this morning. And if there were any deer in those barren mountains, surely it would be open season on does.

He propped his gun by the door and took his cigarettes out of his white dress-shirt pocket. "Toork-ishy," he said about the blended tobacco, and smiled. (He was fascinated that I would be going to Turkey in several days.) We each picked a cigarette out of the small package. Fingers cradling his lighter, he pushed one side of the pop-up top and lit us up, then set the lighter vertically on the table for my observation, the acrid smoke swirling around the two-inch cylinder affixed to a square-edged tower of equal size. Its crown was slotted all around and with a movable band for regulating the air. Etched with varying designs—cross-hatching, tiny squares, vertical grooving—sections of it could be retracted or opened to reveal meticulously fitted compartments housing flint and wick, fuel storage and adjustable parts. Apparently tin, it possessed a certain elegance, outside and in.

After Uncle Raffaele went farther up into the mountains on his fox hunt, I straightened my clothes and things, tried in vain to communicate with my great aunt (she was tight with words), then left the meager two-room dwelling connected with dozens of others lining the sides of an irregular, steep-sloping stone-and-mortar pathway. I wanted to see the village from the top. Every so often a thick, rectangular stone embedded in the path required a long step upward. Small children played at several of these stones; at one of them a little girl in a flimsy dress sat, then slid off onto the path, surely scraping her tender legs but laughing all the way. Soon I had to move aside for a bent man leading a donkey up the hill. The donkey let go, and two women rushed out of opposite-side dwellings, scooped up what Uncle Raffaele told me later was valuable fertilizer, gave me a not-too-friendly glance, and retreated into their darkened doorways with their prize. After I saw the view from the top, I turned around and carefully negotiated my way down the hill, for the stones were worn slick. Taking a long step down was especially tricky; each time, I turned my leading foot and braced against the incline.

When Uncle Raffaele returned, he stood in the doorway, holding his rifle in his left hand. His mouth slightly open, he threw his head back and, proclaiming, *"Niente"* (Nothing), brushed the fingers of his right hand out from under his chin, a gesture I interpreted as *so what?* After he hung up the rifle, he selected two empty bottles and saying, *"Andiamo"* (Let's go), led the way to the wine shop, where the only rotund man I'd seen so far filled the bottles and we sat talking and smoking cigarettes over a couple of full glasses. Soon other men joined us, saying they wanted to meet "*il Americano.*"

But it was clear to me after a while that they really wanted to spend time with Uncle Raffaele, whom in their dialect they called Rah-hay.

"*Eh, Rah-hay, che pensa per...?*" (What do you think about...?)

They asked his advice on personal matters, discussed the weather which never seemed to change, and glanced at me as they talked in muted tones. By the second bottle, the talk (I could tell, but could not follow it) turned to politics and the poor conditions of the village and the province. A wiry man, his head thick with black ringlets, reported that his Grundig short wave.... I caught only "*i comunisti.*" By that time everybody was so animated it was difficult to perceive true seriousness without a cooler source of information. In a way, I'd have welcomed a report of world news; in another, I was content to be suspended up there with the music of the language of my ancestors playing all around, even if I did not always completely understand what was being said.

~

Now, my visit on its final day, I walked with my great uncle (a sort of commoners' squire), as he and I were greeted many times and those I had come to know bade me *buona fortuna*. We spent much of that afternoon visiting relatives, numbering to a small portion of the village.

After our last night together of laughing in that god-awful bed so unfriendly to a human back, I gave Uncle Raffaele a carton of Winstons and, telling him that I wouldn't be needing *lire* where I was going, convinced him to take my extra. Aunt Carmella seemed by her bare smile to encourage his acceptance. Then I gave her an awkward hug, and Uncle Raffaele and I walked down the hill to the *piazza*.

I went into the domed church, lit a candle, kneeled, and said a prayer. Then we went to the wall where, half a century before, the villagers had waved to the eighteen-year-old girl with one eye, who was to become my grandmother, on the morning of her journey to America. Uncle Raffaele recounted the scene as we looked out over the barren mountains.

"*Mai piu*," he added after a pause, his features sharp like hers, a mirthful mouth and at his eyes tears ready to spill. "We never saw her again."

He was not well. His face bones shone angular, and he hunched his knobby shoulders, coughing, as I recalled what he had suffered as a soldier during World War One.

I asked a passing man to snap a picture of us, and he did. After we lit cigarettes, I handed Uncle Raffaele the silvery Zippo and told him I wanted him to have it. He flipped the top and snapped it closed, then handed me his cylindrical pop-up of antiquarian charm. It was shiny, then. Now, fifty years later, I have it still. While it has lost most of its luster and the tiny etched lines have darkened, and it has had no wick or fuel in it for forty years (I haven't smoked for twenty) and my Uncle Ralph (as I have come to call him in my thoughts) is many years dead, I see in it, as it stands upright before me, an ironic sign of where I was heading that day; and, for some reason after all these years, I look on the little round bottom of the cylinder to read that it was made in Austria under the commercial brand name Imco Triplex. The word SUPER, in double-lined letters, is prominently last. All of which seems somehow significant, for until this moment I have imagined an Italian craftsman fashioning delicate lines on the small pieces of tin so intricately fitted together. Not until now have I become fully aware of the symbolic gravity of exchanging cigarette lighters with my great uncle: in our case, one little conflagration for another.

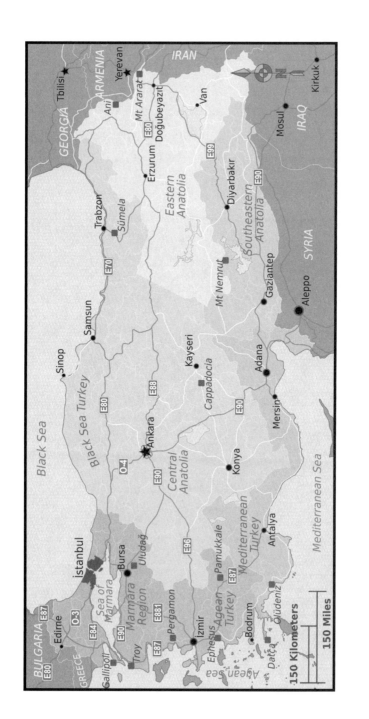

Turkey

URING THE LAST TWO WEEKS, I had not seen a newspaper, had not listened to a radio or seen a television set, had written only postcards to my fiancée and my mother, had received no mail, had not spoken with anyone on the telephone. It was now time to make my way to Cigli Air Base outside Izmir, Turkey, where I had been assigned as a nuclear-weapons maintenance officer.

I walked from the upper village to lower Gimigliano and caught the bus to Catanzaro, at the inner top of Italy's high heel. There, I boarded a train to Brindisi, then went by hydroplane to southern Greece, to Athens by train, and by plane to Izmir (old Smyrna). Finally, I was driven to the air base.

It was a bus ride into the Bible.

Along the way, a woman in black led a donkey, trailing a man by several yards. On the other side, an old man pulled a cart. In the rear-view mirror I saw the bus driver's lips moving slightly, and wondered if he might be silently cursing me for being the only passenger. (It was Friday, October 19, 1962, the last day I would ever be twenty-three, and I felt as if I were growing older by the mile.) A camel strutted before us on its springy feet, and the driver stopped, fingering something like a rosary in his right hand. It was my first camel-sighting and I wanted to see it more closely, but I thought better of asking the seriously mustached driver to wait while I got out to take a picture. The camel crossed, and I turned to see its big lips moving as if it were telling the man pulling on its bit to ease up or it would bite his head off.

We rode on another few miles through the treeless landscape of sand and rocks, and then the isolated air base hove into view on the left, a minaret rising up out of it like a large roman candle, a community of houses on the right resembling a small American suburb with a sapling here and there and a scattering of meager lawns.

I checked into the Bachelor Officers' Quarters (BOQ), a two-bedroom apartment sans kitchen with tiled floors and large windows in a spacious living room with a view of the base on one side and a walkway overlooking a quadrangle on the other. It would be home for thirteen months, and no roommate as yet. Which suited me fine. I had books to read, I had a new Olympia portable typewriter I'd bought at the AFEX in Wiesbaden, and I intended to get started on something that had inspired me in Italy; but when I looked out over the desert-like base, I felt the pull of the Officers' Club.

There, I drank and rubbed shoulders with variously uniformed missilemen and pilots, support personnel and civilian engineers, the buzz among them mixed in with what appeared to be, oddly, a forced camaraderie. Apparently, our Defense Readiness Condition, usually at peacetime's DEFCON 5, had been elevated to 4, and everybody in Operations and Headquarters had a different reason for it.

A large colonel came in, and soon I was introduced to him—the base commander—as "the new arrival in Special Weapons."

"Big job you have, son. The free world is depending on you." He had a drink in his hand by then, and he raised it; we all followed his lead, as he bellowed: "What's the name of the game, men?"

"Erection!" they sang out in unison, tossing their drinks down as if we were in a saloon in the Old West, while I pondered the irony (as I had taken it) about what I might have to offer the free world.

After a while, as the colonel was leaving, he stumbled over a bar stool and had to be helped to his quarters.

Later, it came to me that my birthday was tomorrow, and I told the fellow beside me.

"It *is* tomorrow," he said, and they raised a toast to me, and then another, and another. By the time I was twenty-four years and one-twelfth-of-a-day old, I could have used some help getting to my quarters as well. But I was pretty much on my own.

The next day, I reported to the Chief of Special Weapons Maintenance, a dandyish major with a small mustache who had nothing good to say about Turkey and Turks except for their inexpensive exquisite rugs and their affordable ornate jewelry, which he had been buying in quantities as large as the Status of Forces Agreement, and Turkish law, would allow him to take with him to the States. He said straight off that I would be, unofficially, Acting Company Commander, responsible to him but completely in charge. He said that he would tell the men that when I spoke, I spoke for him. He didn't want to have to go to any of the missile sites again. He was on his last tour of duty—his wife and two daughters were with him—and he just wanted to get the rest of his three-year hitch over with and retire.

And so, on my twenty-fourth birthday, like a present, some seventy enlisted men and NCOs and the re-entry vehicles and warheads for fifteen Jupiter missiles—each with an equivalent explosive capacity of 1.45 megatons of TNT, or one hundred atomic bombs of the size that had destroyed Hiroshima—had been given over to my supervision for their storage and maintenance behind multiple fences, and their transportation to and assembly at the missile sites.

"PMA," Major Jacks said, "and you'll get your rewards."

He turned me over to a sergeant and some airmen, we sat in a small lounge area, and after a while they began to smile as scratching and snorting sounded down the hallway. Suddenly something turned into the doorway and…jumped on my lap!

I was staring into the snout and budding tusks of a wild boar.

"That's Jacky," one of the men said, "a baby we found out in the hills with no mama."

I touched his skull with a fingertip. "Hello, there, Jacky."

One of the men took him off my lap. "We named him after the old man."

Another one said, "Now you're the old man, we'll name the next one after you."

"I don't know," I said. "I'm too young to be the old man."

The next day I asked Tech Sergeant Bailey, who had been taking USAFI correspondence courses in French for years and planned to study and live in France when his hitch was up—and who really ran things around there—"What's PMA, Sarge?"

"Protect My Ass, sir. Yes, sir, I will."

Over the next two days, Sergeant Bailey took me in the company pickup truck over steep, unpaved roads with no guard rails to two of the five missile sites, three missiles to each site, that had been constructed to within 150 miles of the Soviet border, and had become operational only six months ago. The first of the many place names that would stay with me began to crop up in Sergeant Bailey's briefing: Akhisar, Manisa, Adana. As we passed through isolated villages, children waved and yelled. "Amerr-ican! Amerr-ican!" Mustached men and veil-faced women looked at us with dark, mysterious eyes. I could not tell by those eyes if we were being looked upon as intruders or allies.

The five missile sites, identical in layout, were many miles distant from one another. While I would "inspect" only two of them that day and the next, I would be pulling launch-control officer duty on all of them, and sooner than I knew. The first one we went to, LP-4—the one second closest to the Soviet border—was quite far from the base. Five American officers and ten airmen—and an equal number of Turks—were stationed at each site. The three missiles and their launch emplacements were positioned several hundred yards apart. Twenty vehicles served as ground support equipment for each emplacement: generator and power-distribution trucks, short- and long-range theodolites, hydraulic and pneumatic trucks, a trailer-truck loaded with four thousand gallons of liquid oxygen.

"Lox," Sergeant Bailey called it. "That trailer over there"—he pointed to a big one—"contains six thousand gallons of RP-1." When I didn't say anything, he added: "Liquid fuel."

Double fences enclosing attack dogs ran the peri-
meter of each site. Turkish guards manned the gates
around the clock. A one-story barracks housed
American airmen and American and Turkish officers on one end, and Turkish soldiers on the other. The missiles with nose cones mounted—sixty
feet long, eight feet in diameter—were stored erect
on the launch pad and could be "de-erected" for
nose cone maintenance and replacement. The bottom third of the missiles were encased in what
was called a "flower petal shelter": dozens of pan-
els shaped like large artichoke leaves, for inclement-
weather servicing. A trailer served as launch-control
operations center for an American officer and two

crewmen and their Turkish counterparts, each with a key around his neck.

When, after inspecting LP-3, we returned to the base at the end of the second day, October 22, we learned that, shortly before President Kennedy announced it to the world, the Soviet Union had installed secret missile bases in Cuba; and that, after weighing several options, the President had ordered what he termed a naval "quarantine" of the island ninety miles from Florida. (Apparently, to have called it what it was—a blockade—would have constituted an act of war.) Earlier, U.S. military alert had been set at DEFCON 3. It appeared that we were creeping closer to war, and that, if numbers have any logic beyond their own, we were halfway there.

That day, I now know, the control of Squadron I at Cigli Air Base, under NATO II, was turned over to Turkey as host nation, as, over two years before, thirty Jupiter missiles—installed in a place with a lovely name, Gioia del Colle, Joy of the Hills—had been turned over to Italy under NATO I.

The next day, October 23, I was scheduled for launch-control officer duty at LP-I, the missile site nearest the air base. As Sergeant Bailey drove me there early in the morning, he seemed to be brooding.

He was around forty, a tough, lean, no-nonsense tech sergeant who seemed, especially today, to be carrying a heavy weight; and, now that I think back on it, he was: me. As he briefed me during the relatively short drive on the duties I was soon to assume, I wished that he were the officer going into the trailer as he let me off and said he would pick me up at twenty-hundred tomorrow, in thirty-six hours.

I entered the launch-control trailer and reported to the young, blond captain from Operations Company. He introduced me and the Turkish Air Force officer, Lieutenant Yarcan, who would be my counterpart. I said, *"Merhaba"*; he said, "Hello." The captain then gave me the book of instructions marked TOP SECRET, including a plastic-covered single page he called "the idiot sheet," and the chain with the key from around his neck. As I put it over my head, he led me through the procedures I should follow if word came to arm and launch the nuclear warheads.

"Hold your own, Lieutenant."

"Yes, sir," I said.

He shook hands with Lieutenant Yarcan, and left us alone.

The Turkish lieutenant, in his heavy, dark woolen uniform, smoked acrid cigarettes while I puffed

American Turkish blends, the currents of our smoke meeting like silently clashing, ephemeral dragons between us, and we occasionally eyed each other. As I made a motion to convey that I needed to read the instructions, a confusion of fear gripped me: What if the order came to arm the missiles now, and to stand by for launch? And what if they *were* launched? With fifteen to twenty minutes notice, the three missiles from this site, along with the twelve from the other four sites, would be propelled to an altitude of up to 400 miles, and travel within a range of 1,500 nautical miles. As I understood the procedure, if we were called upon to insert the keys, install the buddy-system activation codes, and launch the missiles, the order would come from the base commander, who, with the Officer of the Day, would provide those activation codes to the launch-control officers, Lieutenant Yarcan and me.

The next night, October 24, when Sergeant Bailey let me off at the BOQ, I was greeted by a short, pudgy cherub named Aaron Gottlieb, who had been on base for six months and would be my roommate. He was in Supply Company and seemed about as unsuited to the military as a large part of me was, and so I tried to engage him in his interests, of which I had little knowledge: biology and horticulture.

Soon, we went to the O. Club, where I had a Manhattan (Aaron didn't drink) and ate a late dinner. We then moved into the bar, mingling among missilemen and supply types. We yakked on, a poker game broke out, and I sat in on the first of many late-night and all-weekend sessions.

Around two A.M., when I had three to a straight flush in seven-card stud and three cards coming, Little Moe (what several men had been calling Aaron) whacked his forehead with the heel of his hand.

"God! I forgot to tell you: Headquarters called earlier. You have O. D. tomorrow." He added, "Officer of the Day," as if I wouldn't know.

I could not fathom the thought that, with all that was going on, a NATO missile command in Turkey had, apparently, been waiting for me to come and assume such awesome duties, one after another. Somebody took over my poker hand, telling me he'd split if we won, and Aaron and I went to our quarters, and to bed.

In what seemed like minutes, I woke to Aaron's tooting a make-believe bugle and yelling: "Reveille! Go grab some S.O.S. You've got to get going, buddy-goy."

After coffee and cigarettes, I made my way to Headquarters, where the outgoing O. D., a former pilot with only half a face, said, "Boy, you look twice as bad as me." Then he briefed me on my duties and signed over a thin notebook—the Book of Codes— to me, telling me that if I was going to sleep be sure to strap the book to my chest. As he left, an airman locked me in the room with nothing but a small table, cot, and chair, a bathroom and a few Air Force magazines. I sat and flipped mindlessly through the pages to keep from considering the power of the thin book before me and the results if the codes were entered into the warheads and the missiles were launched.

Later, when the airman came to see if I wanted anything, I asked for a pencil and paper and began writing disjointed notes. When, later still, he brought a plate of food, and while I ate, the code book in front of me on the table, I continued writing notes, letting them lead wherever they would. Finally, I lay face-down on the cot, the code book strapped to my chest. I did not sleep but still dreamed, in a kind of daymare of riotous, elusive images.

During the long afternoon, I did push-ups, wrote verses, and reviewed the manual. When the airman brought more food, I asked him if he'd heard anything about what was happening in Cuba. He said he had not. I picked over the food and, fixing the code book to my chest, finally went to sleep. Old Testament horrors came in graphic sleep-dream this time. If something were or were not done, it would be the end. I knew this in the dream because it was not only my Lost Dream, in which I was always late and looking for a way to somewhere or a way out of a place. Apocalypse was at hand. I *needed* to find my way in that dream, *or I would not wake up.*

"Sir! Sir! DEFCON 2! The base commander is waiting for you in his office." I rolled off the cot in the dark, and the airman, shining a flashlight, helped me untie the code book, led me to the darkened base commander's office, and left, closing the door. I did not know what time of night or day it was. I saw a flashlight and went to it, and found the base commander, kneeling by the open safe.

"DEFCON 2," he said, "one step from launch, and the goddamn lights are out." He yelled for the airman to check on the generator, but he was not going to wait for full light, I could see. "It's all come down to us, son."

At that moment, I did not know, 1,500 of our strategic bombers were on alert worldwide; 200 were in the air at all times; 145 intercontinental ballistic missiles—the vaunted ICBMs that made the 1945 atomic bombs seem like firecrackers—were targeting the Soviet Union.

"Are you ready with your codes, Lieutenant?"

Now I know—then, I must have sensed—that the Soviets, the Cubans, the Americans would all know soon after any nuclear missile was fired anywhere. There would be no such thing as a single missile launched by any one side, for all sides would fire all they had against one another and World War Three would begin and end in a matter of hours: The Last World War, as I think of it now.

In the brief lull since the colonel's question—not, curiously, an order—I heard him, a man too large for uniformed service, breathing heavily. As we knelt before the dark maw of the safe, his knee joint creaked, and in a moment I heard from out of my past, *Don't let go.* Years ago, I had taken aim with my slingshot at a high-up window of a school building on a Saturday, then thought for some time, not so much to fix my aim as to make the choice of whether or not to release the sling. As soon as I'd let go, I wished the rock back, trying to undo the decision by telling myself, even then, *don't let go.* But the rock had already sailed true, and cost my mother's hard-earned waitress tips to restore.

Now, the world was in the balance, and there would be no restoration. For whatever reason—paternal, fraternal, fears of his own—the colonel did not press me; he'd maybe wished a rock or a fist back himself.

The colonel before me, the President, the world— no, I was not ready with any codes. My hands tight on either side of the book, I pressed it to my chest... and began to quake. It occurred to me, even in the state I was in, that I might withhold the goddamn codes, even if President Kennedy had sent the order himself! Hell, no, I thought I said...but I hadn't. I'd just shaken my head vigorously in the dark, unseen.

Suddenly, the telephone rang its stark double-rings at the same time that the airman banged the door open, yelling, "Stand down, sir! Stand down, sir! We've gone back to DEFCON 3!"

The world now knows that complications over the next two days sent us even closer to the nuclear brink than we had been on October 25. Kennedy and Khrushchev exchanged slow, heated, often unreliable communications, with Castro on the side agitating

for confrontation and even a first strike against the
U.S. On the twenty-sixth, with Soviet missiles fully operational in Cuba, Robert Kennedy and Soviet
Ambassador Dobrynin agreed that, if the Soviet missiles in Cuba were withdrawn, the U.S. would not
invade Cuba.

President Kennedy would not agree to any im-
mediate quid pro quo concerning the Jupiters in
Turkey. Since, like the Soviets, we had "secret missile
bases," and the site nearest to the Soviet border was
perhaps only two times the distance to it as that
between Cuba and Florida, it seems now that the
demands President Kennedy had made of Premier
Khrushchev might reasonably have been made of the
U.S. by the Soviet leader. It is now known, however,
that Kennedy, shortly after he became President, had
ordered the Jupiters' continuing installation termi-
nated and all missiles removed from Turkey. Later,
he had been furious to find out that they were still
there.

On the twenty-seventh, however, an American
U-2 spy plane accidentally flew into Soviet air space,
another was shot down over Cuba, killing its pilot,
and Kennedy considered destroying all surface-to-air
missiles on the island. He also ordered that all U.S.

missiles with atomic warheads be defused, so that he alone would be able to arm them. It was the most perilous day of the crisis, yet my fear was somewhat lessened by knowing that President Kennedy, at all times, controlled what in war parlance was known as the "football": a briefcase carried by an aide near him at all times containing the codes—in effect, the nuclear trigger.

One of Khrushchev's letters arrived hours after being sent, and in several disarranged parts; another seemed to contradict the first. It seems, now, that Khrushchev himself was not certain about who was in charge. Kennedy called up reserve troops, ordered ships and a 145,000-man invasion force configured, and prepared for over 1,000 attack sorties for the first day.

All was in place for the Cuban catastrophe that had been building. Kennedy had only to give the order. What he did, though, was to send his brother to meet with Dobrynin again. And so the tension continued around the clock.

Then, on the twenty-eighth, on Radio Moscow, Khrushchev announced his intentions to dismantle the missiles in Cuba but made no public demand that the U.S. do the same in Turkey.

Since the failed U.S.-backed attempt to invade Cuba at the Bay of Pigs, along with an ongoing U.S. plot to assassinate Castro, the missiles in Cuba were like deadly pawns set in place to protect their Cuban ruler—and symbols of a larger, even more dangerous, situation in Berlin. That is why there had been forty thousand Soviet troops in Cuba during the crisis, to be employed in the event of a U.S. invasion there, and why Castro had tactical nuclear weapons he was authorized by Khrushchev to use in defense of the island.

Like all but very few people, I knew none of this then.

A few weeks after the crisis, Major Jacks—that is, I; then, in turn, Sergeant Bailey—was given orders to begin planning for the dismantling and removal of all Jupiter warheads from the five Turkish sites and from storage at the air base. The actual removal was to be done in April, the six-months' lapse, it is now clear, in keeping with the U.S. insistence that we were not actually making a "trade" with the Soviets.

I'd pulled a scant eight days of my assignment in Turkey, aging from twenty-three to twenty-four the first day, and from twenty-four to something beyond mere years in the week that followed. I had a full year and a month to go.

Relieved of the pressures of October, in my off-time I went by base bus to see the sights of Izmir. Its sounds were equally exotic, punctuated by shrill chanting from time to time when criers mounted the minarets in calls to prayer. My first Biblical impression faded into boyhood's book-and-movie memories of *A Thousand and One Nights*—but with dozens of aromas and odors. I made my way through the streets ripe with roasting pistachio nuts and shish kebabs, incense and bread loaves and dates, cedar- or camphor-sweet smoke. Artisans and merchants displayed their puzzle rings and meerschaum pipes, alexandrites and filigreed silver; stacks of sumptuous, hand-tied rugs; shiny lamb carcasses hanging in windows as if being cured by crazed flies. Men smoked water pipes in *chai* shops; boys emerged from them swinging three-string-supported trays carrying filled, gravity-defying glasses. Throughout my walks, I had a dull foreboding (from movies simulatedly set in Morocco and Arabia, no doubt) that if I strayed down an alleyway or through a side street into the wrong doorway, I might never be heard from again. The apprehension was dispelled as I saw other Americans from the air base laughing and chatting with the merchants at their shops and carts.

We'd been cautioned to respect the customs of our host country, a strong and faithful NATO ally. While Kemal Ataturk, father of modern Turkey, had led a segment of the country into the progressive age, the old customs, largely those of the overwhelming Moslem majority, prevailed at the time—not in downtown Izmir, perhaps, but in the outlying areas and provinces. A few American women and girls wore provocative clothing, and every now and then had to be asked to dress more modestly. It was said that an American was at that very moment rotting in a Turkish prison, and I thought of the Prisoner of Chillon. That was topped over drinks one night with the story of an American woman who was smuggled out of the country in a mailbag before she was to go to court for some "crime" that varied with alternate tellers.

I felt more anachronistic than ever as I tooled along to Ephesus in my red-and-black Plymouth Belvedere that had finally arrived from the States. All windows down, I recited—at times declaimed at full volume— Paul's Letter about love (although the *agape* type): "…I

am become as sounding brass or a tinkling cymbal...."
(I addressed it to the Ephesians, since I was going
to Ephesus; my present, retroactive apologies to the
Corinthians.) I roamed among the ruins, a chaos of
stones with scarcely a trace remaining of the Temple
of Artemis (I preferred her Roman name, Diana),
one of the Seven Wonders of the World. Finally,
I walked to the top of the amphitheatre, an enormous bowl of tiered slab stones, and imagined what
I might have seen all those centuries ago.

In an hour or so, tired of all the history and ruins,
I drove back to the base. I'd go see the house of Mary,
not far from where I was now, some other time.

~

Mustafa, a teenaged busboy at the Officers' Club, told me about the camel fights held during December-February, "when," as he said, "men camels get in the good old mood." It was my chance to see them up close, sneak some pictures, so in February I went to a fight a mile or so from what was called NATO Beach, on the Aegean. Scattered crowds formed on a gradual hillside, green and stony, surrounding a large, flat field of sand and rocks within which men squatted as in a huddle near their camel. Other men, some wearing colorful turbans, several in elaborately and colorfully designed sweaters, held their camel's halters and ropes.

I gesture-asked a woman wearing a common head scarf if I could take a picture of her little girl in a red coat and white scarf. When she didn't react, I put a benign look on my face and took the picture at the same time that a large man in a long, black coat turned his dark and searing face to me. His head went up slightly and he jerked it, closing his eyes briefly and making the mouth sound I knew well but could not actually hear: *tsk*. As I walked among the crowd, then finally moved closer down to see the dromedaries better, without sighting I snapped some pictures from the camera strung around my neck, dangling to my belt. I thought I was being so surreptitious, they'd never know. Now, I see myself, harmless enough, but nonetheless an intruder who could not understand that not everyone wants to be in the camera's eye.

Especially not the camels, although having their pictures taken was the least of their displeasure. For here they came, both feet on the right side stepping forward together alternately with both on the left, giving them a bounce. Men manipulated them—two males in rut (if that is what being "in the good old mood" might be called for camels)—with ropes tied to their necks. Sumptuously ornamented in those gorgeous coverings so common in Turkey that even

grain sacks are works of some art, and gleaming with metalwork and bells, the two wrestlers were being presented as bridegrooms, their backgrounds and records apparently being announced as they then were taken to the ring in a show of pomp and ceremony. The stars' heads raised high on their long, curved necks, they seemed to strike a haughty pose, but it was not arrogance. Their eyes had to be raised to see under the heavy lashes and lids. Taken with the large toadstool of a nose with a wide slit on either side, the long parabola of a mouth gashed at the upper middle like a hare's, and the pompadoured head, they were unlikely warriors.

Until the little cutie was brought on. The rivals eyed her up and down, then began prancing, circling, provoking each other. And the raging began. Seemingly feinting little boxing steps every now and then, they grunted and foamed at the mouth, and suddenly lunged at each other. The crowd called to their favorites—what I heard as Jommee and Akkar—and swayed, faces serious, for clear views. The combatants would surely have brought blood, but throughout it all handlers held a pair of restraining ropes on each camel to keep them from seriously hurting each other, and as protection for the spectators,

to whom the camels seemed somehow eerily cued.
At a harsh rebuke from a disgruntled man, Jommee
went for him but was restrained. Once, when a woman sang out praise to Akkar, he stopped, raised his

head higher, and gave a ruminative chew on his cud. He might have been one in a line of camel wrestlers in the Great Amphitheater at Ephesus, with 25,000 spectators and *Oedipus the King* the next billing.

Jommee took advantage of the moment and tripped Akkar, but Akkar rose from his front knees more quickly than I thought he could and began to kick and buck and spit. Suddenly, he whirled and thrust his head between Jommee's legs and pushed and jerked mightily until, at last, Jommee went down and over, his back touching ground in what was evidently the equivalent of a pin. The judges stopped the bout, Akkar was pulled away from his vanquished foe and proclaimed the winner, and I could see his long lashes shading his eyes as dozens of tiny mirrors sewn on his blanket twinkled and winked in the sun and he looked over his shoulder for his prize, his love.

But he was now being led from the field, away from her. As the champ's handlers praised their boy, their rapturous faces upturned to him, a balloon-sized bubble of drool oozed from Akkar's mouth and dropped, breaking over a man's ecstatic face and slithering down his shoulders.

(A Turkish woman, a classical musician, has told me recently that Izmir is a clean, cosmopolitan city and that camel "wrestling"—she called it—is no longer legal. She added that a camel cannot be seen except in places where tourists are given rides.)

Winter had come and gone without fanfare, and a spring, such as I'd never known, now followed. It rained, but not much seemed to grow.

During the next weeks I held meetings with Sergeant Bailey and the crews that would be removing the warheads in April. The major had "important business" in Izmir most of that week, which meant that he was loading up on more carpets and jewelry. Often I played late-night poker and drank gambling's attendant nectar served always by one of the many pleasantly accommodating Turkish waiters we called *garçon*. On a Saturday afternoon, I caught up on my laundry, packed a sandwich and some drinks in my small cooler, and went to see what I had come to think of as the Tree. Aaron had heard about it from one of his men.

It was about ten miles away. While it did not compare to my favorite oak and a particular pine (that may or may not have existed), both in Virginia, it was large and beautiful, the best and largest I'd seen so far in Turkey. I sat in its shade for more than an hour, imagining that it was one of the mythical American chestnuts that had once covered the hills and coves of Appalachia, their creamy blossoms cascading in spring like giant ice cream cones. I'd never seen one, but I'd come upon a picture in a library and, having heard about them from an old woman who'd seen the living tree, turned on the picture of it in my head. The blight had transformed them to blackened eighty-foot poles before I was born, and they had long since been milled into lumber impervious to rot: fences and furniture for the ages.

The exact locations of the missile sites we traveled to during April to remove the nose cones containing the nuclear warheads from the Jupiters and return them to the base for dismantling and shipment out of the country are, after several decades, de-classified information. Which is neither here nor there: I cannot recall them anyway. Place names on the way to the sites have remained with me: Trabzon, Incirlik, Karamürsel. I liked the last best: Its syllables composed a little song.

On a typical overnight round-trip, Sergeant Bailey drove our pickup, following the two-and-a-half-ton truck with the nose cone containing the warhead. I

rode a sort of modern shotgun, as I thought of it, a .45
automatic strapped to my waist. The Turkish Military
Police led and followed in pickup trucks each of the
fifteen convoys we made over the next two weeks. The
roads and wooden bridges seemed to me always ready
to wash out or cave in. Ed Rollins, who took every
third or fourth convoy, had a close call on what he
called in the company bay area one day "a bastard of
a curve." Airman First Class Stover, a grizzled hardass
with a full, curly mustache, topped that with his story
about another wooden passenger bus that had gone
into a ravine that day. The men talked often, with some
exaggeration, about the drivers of the rickety buses
going *çok çabuk* over the treacherous roads while they
fingered what the men called their worry beads and
repeated in silent Turkish prayers, "Allah will provide."

On one return trip, I was anticipating a particular stretch of road we had covered on the way to the
site. Now loaded, after a double-switchback mount-
ing a sharp incline, we leveled off some. Then, after
another rise, I looked down. It was dry here. Dust
and dirt began to fill the cab, and we rolled up the
windows. Sergeant Bailey turned on the windshield
wipers that struggled and vibrated but cleared some

of the glass. I could hear rocks clipping off under the truck's wheels, hitting metal, and when the dust clouds cleared to my right I saw the rocks rolling down the mountain. Above us, all but the lead vehicle hidden in dust cover, the rest of the convoy was making its way. When a passage cleared, I saw the nose cone on the truck ahead of us, reddish-brown now but holding firm in its straps.

Later, as we were going through a village, the truck carrying the warhead stalled, then stopped. While people came, in few numbers at first, to see the large nose cone, I took up what I figured was guard position. The Turkish MPs let it be known that while I was in command of the convoy, they were in charge of its safety, and they set up a ring of guards around the truck, the villagers coming in greater numbers now until a small crowd circled the MPs. Anxious faces stared into the center of the scene, and I felt foolish with a gun strapped to my waist, as if I dared dare anyone to make a move. The ranking MP pretended to address me, but he really asked Sergeant Bailey to concentrate on the malfunction so we could get out of there. Sergeant Bailey and a mechanic took care of it in short order.

~

When my company's part in the removal operations was completed, I spent my days filing reports on the logistical operations and writing personnel effectiveness reports. I took a full day to work on Sergeant Bailey's evaluation. Luckily, my young clerk typist, Airman Dexter, from Georgia, was serious and exacting. My editing and re-drafting, no matter how minor, he took as opportunities to learn. And when the heavy work was over and our mission changed to supporting fighter planes, he asked my permission to marry a beautiful, young Turkish woman, as he showed me her picture. I was his commanding officer, his senior by only three or four years in age, but by legal decades in rank. I wasn't going into the cautionary speech about different cultures and all that. I asked him one question, or rather made one statement: "You love her, I can see."

Airman Dexter smiled seriously. He was handsome, clean-cut, boyish, and I had no doubts but that he would do well with his life. "Yes, sir," he said. "I surely do."

Brash, young fighter pilots began showing up in their flight fatigues (some non-pilots called them pajamas, behind their backs) at the O. Club, and the bar-andflyboy bullshit flew. They ordered depth charges—mugs of beer with a jigger of cognac dropped in (shot glass and all)—then chugged them and played liars' dice for the tab. They sprayed gin from their mouths across high-flaming Zippos, creating mini-afterburners. How they loved their afterburners! As they replayed the day's dogfights with their hands, they seemed to be orchestrating their supremacy over those of us who still wore impotent missile badges. I laughed at one when he spilled a drink, and he wanted to fight me, but as he came at me his buddy calmed him down. And soon that buddy, Captain Leonard Fiege, a wild-man fighter pilot from Bayfield, Wisconsin, became my roommate when Aaron returned to the States. Everybody called him Fig.

One day the following week, driving into the city to meet some American NATO officers at the Izmir Officers' Club, as I passed the now familiar sight of a donkey led by a pantalooned woman, head and lower face veiled, trailing a man in a dark Western coat, I felt a current of shame for our disparity. After lunch at the club, a purely social occasion, I gave in to a boy's eagerness and let him shine my shoes. When I returned to my car, I found it washed and with a smiling, mustached man greeting me: "*Merhaba, Abi.*

Is pretty car, yes?" Something besides the *liras* and
kurus I gave him seemed to pass between us, just as
a crier began the afternoon call to prayer from the
near minaret, like a rocket, and the car-washer hur-
ried away.

For several weeks I had been teaching a USAFI
course in English grammar at the school in the housing area. Several airmen, Dexter among them, were
enrolled. Mustafa, the busboy at the O. Club, had the
kind of personality-cum-humor I had grown up with
in Virginia, and we hit it off, calling each other *Abi*
for a while. Then I began calling him Abs, and told
him to call me Joe. He asked me to teach him "the
English," and I scheduled some private sessions with
him at the club. As a "course" it might have been
called Conversational American English Through
Laughter 101. He was a whiz, picking up slang and
quips as fast as I could throw them, and pitching
back some himself: "Hey, Zho," he might say—then,
trying to imitate my mountain accent, "when you
goin' to teach me some Hillbilly?"

"I'm not a Hillbilly," I told him. "I'm a Mountain
William."

His brow creased. His eyes rolled. "I will think
about that, Zho."

That summer of '63 was a long, lonely respite from the past months between October and June. One day, when I was at Headquarters, I was told that the operator was trying to reach me. After several patches and trunks and voices variously accenting broken English, I heard: "Hello, Joseph." I was lifted out of that loud and busy office, out of Turkey and away from missiles and off roads I might die on at any moment.

It was Julie, my fiancée, calling from Minnesota.

By August, I was already marking time. I had some of the men in our company build horseshoe boxes in the quadrangle, and Father Carlson, from Green Bay, and I won the tournament on Labor Day. I was invited to the house of a Turkish family for a dinner of lamb shish kebab, *pilav* (rice), *ekmek* (bread), and Kavaklidere wine. I went to a concert by the Izmir Symphony Orchestra and a musical play performed by a large cast of women who all revealed themselves, at the end, to be men.

Determined to keep the vow I'd made last year to read a chapter, every night, from my large, red-leather Confraternity and Douay family *Bible*, Rembrandt edition, I had already plowed through long lineages of *begats* which I would have had difficulty remembering even with a clear head. After a late night of poker, I could recall nothing much of those Old Testament heroes and barbarians and innocents in the morning. They merged into one long tragedy, with God a kind of Villain. Inspired by my more recallable reading of non-biblical literature, I began taking what turned out to be jumbled notes for an apprentice novel I would write (and discard) under the title Fall Out for Sunset some few years later. I had by then given up trying to write anything worthy and only read, spending hours under the sun on NATO Beach, gazing out at the Aegean, mythic names playing in my head without clear meaning: Aeneas, Ulysses, Jason. Was it the Phoenicians and the Argonauts who had sailed into battle out there? And then I began imagining what lay beyond, now, in my own time: Greece, Italy, the Straits of Gibraltar, the Atlantic, home. But I'd just finished reading *The Stranger*, and into my head appeared the form of Meursault, walking the beach, unaware that, in a moment, without guilt or repentance, he would kill an Arab for no apparent reason.

How random everything seemed, how vast.

It has been repeated that during the missile crisis one mistake might have precipitated the war that could have ended the world. We now know that several mistakes were made, one of the most potentially devastating of which was the night DEFCON 2—imminent war—had been set by the Chairman of the Joint Chiefs on the night when I had held the Book of Codes tightly to my chest...and President Kennedy had countermanded the order, releasing me from the moment of my most intense distress, and saving the world. The Air Force Chief of Staff had recommended bombing the nuclear emplacements as they were being completed in Cuba, but Kennedy rejected the action. The young President had risen to the task in keeping his generals' assessments and recommended courses of action from prevailing.

And Khrushchev had contained Castro's rage and, in the end, capitulated.

No, it was not that the critical mistake had not been made, but that two men answerable for the fate of the world had chosen—every step of the dangerous way, even during the bumbling—reason over mere action: Premier Nikita Khrushchev, who had seemed a ruffian and a bumpkin, had very likely chosen to jeopardize his position of leadership rather than stay the course to save face; President John Kennedy, who had sent a perilous cold warrior's message to the world in his inaugural address, had kept the lines of communication open to his adversary and had demonstrated that knowledge and intellect are imperatives for one to be President, and cannot be replaced by the use of force alone. Surely, even the Soviet Premier realized as much when he went on Radio Moscow, willing to pay the price.

In my way, then, of seeing, I must have begun to feel that I had done something worthy, especially since I was steadfastly allied with President Kennedy, whose photographed presence and recorded voice never failed to stir my patriotic soul.

Letting a Turkish boy shine my shoes on the streets of Izmir now, I felt less the guilt of compassion. I, too, had shined shoes as a boy on the streets of my home town in Appalachian Virginia. I had washed great numbers of cars at service stations as well. What now passed between me and the shine boys and carwashers was something like an unspoken brotherhood. (I read just the other day that Italians in Tuscany came from Lydia, an old name for Turkey, as Greek historian Herodotus claimed 2,500 years ago. A relative of mine has traced our Calabrese origins to a Greek village, which all sounds to me…possible, if uninteresting: I place little stock in who came from where.)

A sense of well-being overtook me. Our common humanity would prevail, as Kennedy's and Khrushchev's had.

But when, on the evening of the second birthday I marked in Turkey, the criers announced prayers from the minarets in the middle of Ramazan, the Turkish Islamic month of fasting, I listened, and truly heard, the call for the first time. Like a keening, it was, like a lament.

I was troubled, I now see. While I had not by any means grown up sheltered, the past year had left a deposit of harshness beyond the merely personal. It seems to me now that a great, dark shelf of the world had descended during that time of danger I was so ill-prepared for but had had such a central hand in dealing with, and I wonder: What has driven men to sacrifice human blood to their gods in one religion and to drink the symbolic blood of a god in another? What kind of god would command a man to kill his son to prove his loyalty, rather than to refuse to kill him? How can two religions claim preeminence when one slits the throat of the same lamb that is figurative innocence and goodness to the other? What is it in some men that they set dog against dog, cockerel against cockerel, and even the gangly camel against its own? Why this rootedness in bloodlust and vengeance, and all mixed with fervent religious claims of primacy?

The look on Akkar the camel's face, as he was being led away from the field of battle, has stayed with me and seems to speak the answer: *I shall continue to carry your loads, but let me live in peace. I have fought for your degenerate pleasure. Now, let me have my prize, my love, as you promised.*

Gradually, though, the shelf began to lift off and away. By mid-November, the countdown to my date of departure decreasing to single figures, my old idealism began to return. I no longer saw Meursault on the beach in my head, but Jack Kennedy, tanned and smiling, a former Navy man, a hero who had rescued his men at sea.

With three days remaining, Fig went hunting and killed a wild boar and cooked a portion of it on a hot plate in the back hall. For hors d'oeuvres, he was going to serve thin slices of the beeflike pork and add his original embellishments. We had a small bar set up back there as well, and as the guests began arriving I greeted them, Fig mixed the drinks, and Abs, who had asked to help out, served them.

The guests included several American officers and their wives, among them Major Jacks and his

flirtatious wife, Betty, who had a reputation for getting tipsy faster than a sailor on two-hour shore leave;
Ed Rollins, my replacement, and his pretty young
wife, Esther; and the Turkish couple who had invited
me for dinner. The new base commander had said he
would stop by later.

The not-too-large living room was filling up,
people milling around with nowhere, really, to go. I
put a record on the phonograph, and as Dean Martin
began to croon, Betty Jacks was agitating for someone to dance with her. As I went to get a drink for
myself, Esther Rollins was talking about some "cute
popular-music group from England with their dar-
ling long mop-top hair" being "all the rage in the
States"; Fig was drinking from a large glass of bour-
bon; Abs, snapping silent fingers, was singing with
Dean Martin: "Zhe world still is the same. You'll
never change it." I poured some scotch and went to
the bathroom sink and ran water into the glass and
stood, swirling the drink, looking into the mirror—

The music and chatter and loud laughter subsid-
ed into a suspension of sound. I sensed something
like a tangible gasp, then a variety of verbal noises
from choked-off screams to cries of anguish. I went
to the living room. Betty Jacks's face was horrifying,

little screeches like those of a small, hurt animal is-
suing from it. Faces all around had terrifying news
in their eyes.

"Kennedy and Johnson have been shot."

"They mowed down the President and Vice President and Texas governor, and one of their wives."

"The President is dead."

"There's been a coup."

I heard the telephone, barely, and went to it and
stood looking at it, its now urgent double-rings commanding me. Fig rushed in beside me, picked up the
receiver while putting his arm around my shoulders,
then hung up and announced in a voice above the
noise, bringing the room to attention, that those of
us in Operations and Headquarters were to report,
immediately, to our duty posts and wait for word
from the base commander.

As the truth emerged, the portions of days that followed, like gossamer pieces of dream, held me in
equilibrium. Riotous emotions vied with urgent
transcendence. Disturbing pictures came to my head;
others overlaid them with rousing, silent words.
At the memorial service, I served Mass for Father
Carlson and read from Saint Augustine over Turkish

radio: "Too late have I loved thee, O beauty so old and so new." Later, I got in my car and drove without destination. As I went slowly through one village and then another, children came to the side of the road, yelling, "Kenn-e-dee, Kenn-e-dee!" Their elders looked up from where they stood or, if they sat, stood and gave me their sorrowful deference with their faces. I let them see by my eyes, as I could, that we were one in our loss.

I made the turn to Ephesus and drove toward the ruins, then veered off to Selçuk. After a couple of miles I stopped and went to a partially vine-shrouded stone building with an arched doorway resembling a mausoleum. It had been the house of Mary, Mother of Jesus, deemed a holy place by Christians and Muslims alike. She was brought here by Saint John after the Crucifixion, I thought. This is where she died. Recent pictures from military newspapers floated in my head between what I was seeing and thinking and the reality of the past days, and I thought of all the Christmases—the one Christmas, really—and of Mary, ending here in this house of stones, and of Mrs. Kennedy, ashen-faced and stoic in her soiled clothing on the airplane, witnessing the new President's oath-taking.

During the few days before I was to leave, there was talk going around the base of agitation and overthrow, but it apparently had to do with the age-old conflict over Cyprus, or maybe Crete. I knew nothing much about that. By then, I wanted only to be on my way.

On the day of my departure, I was driven to the airport in a staff car escorted by American and Turkish Military Policemen. Soon after the Turkish airliner lifted off, it banked out over the glistening Aegean, where mythic heroes and gods and sailors had clashed for millennia and colossal statues lay, fallen beneath the water, all as if merely a long prelude to the time when warriors might send bombs through the skies, to destroy each other from afar.

J OSEPH MAIOLO WAS BORN IN WEST VIRGINIA, was raised in the Cumberland Mountains of southwest Virginia, and has earned degrees from the University of Virginia (M.A.), the University of North Carolina at Greensboro (M.F.A.), and the United States Naval Academy (B.S.). He is presently a professor of English at the University of Minnesota Duluth, where he teaches literature and fiction writing. His short stories have been published in *The Sewanee Review, Ploughshares, Shenandoah, The Texas Review, The Greensboro Review,* other magazines, and anthologies. Several of his stories and a novella have won national awards, including citation in *The Best American Short Stories,* a Pushcart Prize, two National Endowment for the Arts Literary Fellowships, and three PEN/Syndicated Fiction Awards. Two of the PEN prize stories have been read on National Public

Radio's "The Sound of Writing." Maiolo's work has also received a Bush Artist Fellowship and a Loft-McKnight Award of Distinction in Fiction. "The Girl and the Serpent," an excerpt from his memoir in progress, was published by Beacon Press (Boston) in *Resurrecting Grace: Remembering Catholic Childhoods*. Maiolo has completed two novels, assembled a collection of his short stories, and is revising an Appalachian Virginia memoir.

Maiolo has also co-written the screenplays MY TURKISH MISSILE CRISIS and MOUNTAIN, both currently seeking production, and has written an original screenplay, LEIF'S TUNE. His co-written play, *The Man Who Moved a Mountain*, has enjoyed several productions in southwest Virginia; another play, ONCE ON BUFFALO MOUNTAIN, was dramatically read at the Appalachian Festival of Plays and Playwrights at the Barter Theatre in Abingdon, Virginia. Maiolo has written the treatment for MOVING MOUNTAINS, a video tribute to Robert Childress, in production at the time of this publication.

Additionally, Maiolo has written the lyrics to a suite of four songs—folk, classical, jazz, and rock—which has been performed in concert with orchestra and singers.